Westminster Community Charter School
Library Media Center
24 Westminster Ave.
Buffalo, New York 14215

PREHISTORIC LIFE
FISH

CHRISTA BEDRY

WEIGL PUBLISHERS INC.

Published by Weigl Publishers Inc.
350 5th Avenue, Suite 3304
New York, NY 10118-0069
USA
Web site: www.weigl.com

©2004 WEIGL PUBLISHERS INC.
All rights reserved. No part of this publication may be reproduced, stored in a retrieval system, or transmitted in any form or by any means, electronic, mechanical, photocopying, recording, or otherwise, without the prior written permission of the publisher.

Library of Congress Cataloging-in-Publication Data
Bedry, Christa.
  Fish / by Christa Bedry.
    v. cm. -- (Prehistoric life)
Includes index.
Contents: What is a fish? -- Early history of fish -- A different earth -- Adapting to change -- Finding fish fossils -- Revealing evidence about fish -- Embryologists -- Fish groups -- Fish close-ups -- Life cycle of the fish -- Feeding habits of fish -- Disappearing act -- Fish in folklore and pop culture -- Still digging for fish.
  ISBN 1-59036-112-1 (lib. bdg. : alk. paper)
  1. Fishes, Fossil--Juvenile literature. [1. Fishes, Fossil.] I.Title. II. Series:Prehistoric life (Mankato, Minn.)
  QE851.B384 2004
  567--dc21

2003003968
Printed in the United States of America
1 2 3 4 5 6 7 8 9 0   07 06 05 04 03

Editor Donald Wells
Series Editor Jennifer Nault
Copy Editor Janice L. Redlin
Designer Janine Vangool
Layout Terry Paulhus
Photo Researcher Tracey Carruthers
Consultant Royal Tyrrell Museum of Palaeontology

Photograph Credits
Every reasonable effort has been made to trace ownership and to obtain permission to reprint copyright material. The publishers would be pleased to have any errors or omissions brought to their attention so that they may be corrected in subsequent printings.

Cover: great white shark (**Digital Stock Corp**), landscape (**Photos.com**); **istock photo.com**: page 18 (**Dave Brenner**); **Martha Jones**: pages 9, 15 all, 17TL, 17TM, 17TR, 17BL, 17BR; **Breck Kent**: page 22; **Photofest**: pages 24 (©**Walt Disney**), 25B (©**Universal**); **Photos.com**: pages 1, 6R, 21, 23; **Photovault**: pages 17BM, 19, 29 (**Werhner Krutein**); **Tom Stack & Associates**: pages 10, 11, 12, 13, 14, 16, 20 (**Tom & Theresa Stack**); **Dave Taylor**: pages 5, 7L, 7R, 25T; **Royal Tyrrell Museum/Alberta Community Development**: pages 3, 4, 6L.

Contents

What is a Fish? 4
Early History of Fish 6
A Different Earth 8
Adapting to Change 9
Fish Fossils 10
Revealing Evidence 12
Embryologists 13
Fish Groups 14
Fish Closeup 16
Life Cycle of Fish 18
Feeding Habits of Fish 20
Disappearing Act 22
Fish in Folklore 24
Digging for Fish 26
Further Research 28
Ancient Activity 29
Quiz 30
Glossary 31
Index 32

What is a Fish?

When people talk about fish, they usually refer to an animal with bones and scales. However, the first fish did not have bones or scales. Some of them had bony plates to protect their bodies. Others had a skeleton made of **cartilage**. A few of these kinds of prehistoric boneless fish are still alive today.

Sharks have changed very little over the past 400 million years. They have improved their ability to hunt and eat by evolving better teeth structures and more streamlined body shapes.

Thousands of bony fish **fossils** have been found around the world. The oldest bony fish fossil was found in China.

All fish live underwater, either in oceans, lakes, or rivers. They are **cold-blooded**, use fins to swim, and breathe through gills on the sides of their heads. The gills filter oxygen out of the water. Some fish live in the salty water of oceans, and other fish live in the fresh water of lakes, rivers, and streams. Most fish cannot live in both salt water and fresh water.

FISH FACTS

- The shark is the only fish that has eyelids.
- The largest fish is the whale shark, which grows to more than 50 feet (15 m) and may weigh several tons.
- Whales and dolphins live in the water, but they are not fish. Whales and dolphins have lungs and breathe air. Their young are born alive, just like humans and other mammals.

Early History of Fish

Earth has a long and exciting history. For more than 3.5 billion years, it has been home to many types of animals and plants. Scientists have divided Earth's history into blocks of time called eras. The eras have been divided into periods.

PRECAMBRIAN ERA

Algae fossils

4.6 Billion to 545 Million Years Ago
- During the Precambrian Era, simple life forms first appeared in the seas.

PALEOZOIC ERA

545 Million to 250 Million Years Ago
- Paleozoic means "ancient life." More complex life forms appeared during this era, including fish, insects, land plants, and **reptiles**.
- The Devonian Period, 410 to 354 million years ago, is called the "Age of Fishes."

Trilobite fossils

Different types of plants and animals lived during each of Earth's eras. Fish developed during the Paleozoic Era, which began about 545 million years ago.

Fish evolved from animals that had no backbone. The first fish were called agnathans. Fish with armor on their bodies and jaws, called placoderms, appeared about 400 million years ago. Armored fish evolved from the agnathans. The placoderms became **extinct** about 350 million years ago. Once the placoderms became extinct, the chondrichthians (sharks and rays) and the osteichthians (the bony fish) became the most common types of fish.

MESOZOIC ERA

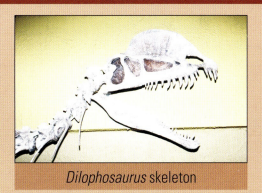

Dilophosaurus skeleton

250 Million to 65 Million Years Ago
- Mesozoic means "middle life." Dinosaurs and birds appeared during the Mesozoic Era. By the end of this era, many of these animals became extinct.

CENOZOIC ERA

65 Million Years Ago to the Present
- Cenozoic means "recent life." All types of mammals began to appear on Earth during the Cenozoic Era.

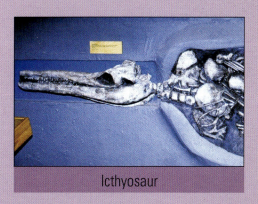

Icthyosaur

A Different Earth

At the beginning of the Paleozoic Era, the supercontinent *Rodinia* split into smaller continents. Toward the end of the Paleozoic Era, the continents moved together and formed the supercontinent *Pangaea*. During the Devonian Period, deserts formed, and the climate became cooler. Glaciers formed, and the sea level dropped. Many types of fish became extinct as a result of the climate change. Some fish **adapted** to the climate change by developing a form of primitive "lungs." Some scientists believe fish with lungs evolved into the first **amphibians**, and later into reptiles.

THE CHANGING CONTINENTS

◆ **Paleozoic Era**
Begins with the breakup of Rodinia

◆ **Paleozoic Era**
Rodinia splits into smaller continents

◆ **Mesozoic Era**
Era begins with continents joining to form Pangaea

Adapting to Change

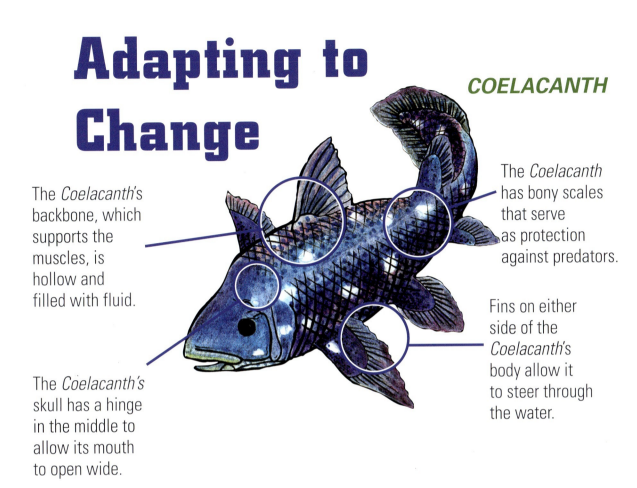

COELACANTH

The *Coelacanth*'s backbone, which supports the muscles, is hollow and filled with fluid.

The *Coelacanth* has bony scales that serve as protection against predators.

The *Coelacanth's* skull has a hinge in the middle to allow its mouth to open wide.

Fins on either side of the *Coelacanth*'s body allow it to steer through the water.

In order to survive climate changes such as drought, some fish learned how to use their fins to move on land. There are still fish in Africa, Asia, and Australia that can walk across land to find food or move to another body of water. Other fish learned to fall into a type of **hibernation** when the climate became too dry. There are several **species** of fish alive today that burrow into the mud and sleep until the climate improves and they can swim again.

Fish Fossils

Many types of fish have been extinct for millions of years. It is not possible to go back in time to see them. It is possible to learn about them by looking at their fossils. Most fish died, and their bodies broke down into simpler parts. Some fish remains became fossils. Fish fossils can be compressions or impressions. Compressions are entire fish skeletons or parts of fish skeletons that were pressed between layers of mud and sand. These layers turned into rock. The trapped fish skeletons and fish parts became fossils. Impressions are marks made by fish scales and skin. Impressions are found in **sedimentary rocks** that were once layers of sand, silt, and mud.

The landscape in the badlands of North America shows the layers of sediment that have built up over time. Many fossils are found in these layers of rock.

Many fish fossils reveal details of scales and fins. Fossils with details of fins have helped scientists understand how some fish may have evolved into amphibians.

HOW FISH FOSSILS ARE FORMED

Paleontologists have found many types of fish fossils. A fossil is created when layers of mud and sand cover the bones of a fish that has died. As time passes, layers of mud build up. The weight of the upper layers of mud pushes down on the lower layers to form solid rock. The remains of the fish become a fossil.

Although many fossils of prehistoric fish have been discovered and studied, it is very rare to find the remains of prehistoric sharks. Sharks do not have skeletons, which means they do not have bones that can become fossils. However, many fossilized shark teeth have been found.

Revealing Evidence

◆　　◆　　◆　　◆　　◆　　◆

Some prehistoric fish species did not become extinct, and scientists are studying them. People thought that a fish called the *Coelacanth* had become extinct long ago. However, in 1938, some **fishers** pulled a live *Coelacanth* out of the ocean. This was a big surprise to scientists. Living *Coelacanths* were able to remain unknown because they live deep in the ocean. Scientists hope that by learning the habits of prehistoric fish species such as *Coelacanths* they will be able to learn more about fish species that are now extinct.

The *Coelacanth* is called a living fossil. *Coelacanth* fossils have been found that are 240 million years old. The youngest *Coelacanth* fossil is 80 million years old. Living *Coelacanths* look much like the fossils.

CAREER LINK

Embryologists

Embryologists study the way animals develop before they are born. Did you know that a bat **embryo** looks very much like a human embryo? Because the embryos of many animals look the same, some scientists believe that studying embryos will give us clues about how animals developed over time. Studying the development of young animals may reveal patterns similar to the evolution of certain species of animals. For example, after a human baby has been in its mother's **womb** for several weeks, it develops gill slits, like fish. These gill slits disappear as the baby continues to develop. To become an embryologist, you need to do well in science classes. You also should develop the language skills necessary for writing reports.

Embryologists sometimes study fossilized embryos to learn about the evolution of animals.

Fish Groups

Fish have been divided into four groups. They are the agnathans, or jawless fish; the placoderms, or armored fish; the chondrichthians, or fish with skeletons of cartilage; and the osteichthians, or bony fish. Some jawless fish still exist, but all of the placoderms have become extinct. Chondrichthians, such as sharks and rays, still exist, but the most common fish alive today is the osteichthians, or bony fish.

Rays first appeared during the Jurassic Period, 205 to 141 million years ago. Because their skeletons are made of cartilage, fossils of complete rays are rare.

AGNATHANS

The first fish were called agnathans, and they appeared about 500 million years ago. They were jawless and usually less than 18 inches (46 cm) long. They lived at the bottom of oceans, lakes, rivers, and streams. Their food was filtered out of water and mud. Most agnathans died out about 360 million years ago. The hagfish is a type of agnathan that is still alive today.

PLACODERMS

Placoderms appeared about 400 million years ago. Most of them were about 3 feet (0.9 m) long, but some grew to be more than 30 feet (9 m) long. Placoderms had armor on their bodies and jaws. Many of these fish were **predators**. Placoderms became extinct about 350 million years ago.

CHONDRICHTHIANS

The first chondrichthians appeared in the Devonian Period. These fish have skeletons made of cartilage. Their teeth are the only bones in their bodies. They are fast swimmers, but if they stop swimming, they sink. Most sharks are predators. The largest sharks, however, filter **plankton** out of the water.

OSTEICHTHIANS

The osteichthians, or bony fish, appeared in the Early Devonian Period. They are the most common fish in the seas, lakes, rivers, and streams of today. Bony fish have an air sac called the swim bladder to help them float in the water. They have a bony skeleton and gills for filtering oxygen from water.

Fish Closeup

Fish have lived since the Paleozoic Era. They began as jawless animals that fed on dead animals and plants. As the jawless fish began to die out, fish with armor on their bodies became the most common type of fish. Most of the armored fish were predators. The armored fish lived for 50 million years and then became extinct. The armored fish were replaced by the bony fish and fish with skeletons made of cartilage. These are the fish that inhabit the waters on Earth today.

Placoderms were armored fish. There were many different types of placoderms, including torpedo-shaped swimmers, flattened bottom-dwellers, and armored box-like fish.

Arthrodires

- The largest predators of the Devonian Period
- Had armor around their heads
- Fed on sharks and other fish
- Up to 20 feet (6 m) long

Coelacanth

- 400 million years old
- Thought to have become extinct with the dinosaurs but were found living in deep ocean water in 1938
- Up to 6.5 feet (2 m) long

Megalodon Shark

- Lived during Cenozoic Era
- An ancient ancestor of the great white shark
- Fossil teeth up to 7 inches (18 cm) long have been found
- Grew up to 52 feet (16 m) long and weighed 48 tons (44 t)

Sturgeon

- Has cartilage and bony protective plates instead of bones and scales
- Has a mouth that acts like a vacuum cleaner and barbels
- Up to 7 feet (2.1 m) long

Carp

- One of the oldest and best known fish in the world Ancient Romans loved this fish enough to **import** it
- Now kept in fish ponds and garden ponds
- Can weigh more than 50 pounds (23 kg)

Razorback sucker

- More than 1 million years old
- Lives in the Colorado River Basin and is an endangered species
- Up to 3 feet (0.9 m) long and can weigh 12 to 13 pounds (5–6 kg)
- Can live to be 40 years old
- Lives and eats on the water's bottom

Life Cycle of Fish

Bony female fish lay their eggs in the water in a protective jelly substance. The male bony fish **fertilizes** the eggs as they float in the water. Sharks lay their eggs inside their body, and the male fertilizes the eggs while they are still inside the female. Some sharks lay the fertilized eggs in the water, and some keep the fertilized eggs inside their bodies until they are ready to be hatched.

Salmon reproduce by spawning. They swim upstream, and the female lays eggs in the riverbed. The male fertilizes the eggs. Salmon are declining in number as a result of dams, destruction of their environment, overfishing, and pollution.

Shrimp first appeared in the Devonian Period, 410 to 354 million years ago.

After an egg is laid outside a fish's body, it usually floats in the water. Often, the jelly substance that protects the eggs glues them to a plant stalk. This keeps the eggs safe. Eggs may be eaten by other fish or insects if they are not secure.

A young fish grows inside an egg. It usually coils around the inside of the egg as it grows longer. It develops inside the egg for 40 hours to 3 months, depending on the type of fish. Eventually, the tail of the young fish breaks through the egg. Now, the young fish can swim, and it begins to eat other small animals, such as small shrimp and insects. The fish grows and develops fins and a tail. When the fish becomes an adult, it will be able to reproduce.

THE UNUSUAL LITTLE SEAHORSE

The seahorse is an interesting fish. This small animal can be found in a variety of sizes and colors on coral reefs. The seahorse has a very unusual way of giving birth. The female lays up to 200 eggs in a special pouch on the front of the male. The eggs are fertilized and **incubated** in this pouch until they are ready to hatch.

Feeding Habits of Fish

In water, plankton serves as the basis of the food web—fish depend on it. Many types of fish and animals, such as jellyfish, shrimp, and snails, eat plankton. Small prehistoric animals and fish that ate plankton became food for larger fish. The larger fish were eaten by even larger fish and animals, such as sharks.

Usually, little fish are eaten by bigger fish, but this is not always the case. Some little fish are fierce predators. Some large fish only eat plankton or plants. Its size is not always a good way to tell where a fish will be in a food web.

The Green River Formation in Wyoming is known for its fossils of fish eating other fish. This type of fossil is rare.

Food Web

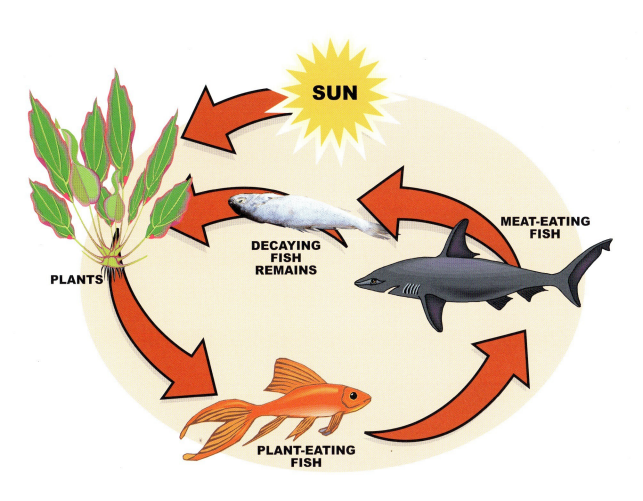

FOOD WEB

Almost every animal that lives in the seas, lakes, rivers, and streams of Earth depends, either directly or indirectly, on microscopic plankton for food. The tiny plants in plankton make their own food by converting the Sun's rays into energy. In turn, some animals eat plankton and plants. These plankton- and plant-eating animals are eaten by meat-eating animals.

Disappearing Act

At the end of the late Devonian Period, 96 percent of the animals living in the shallow seas around the continents disappeared. This extinction opened the way for the bony fish to flourish. Up to this time, there were few bony fish living in the fresh and salt waters of Earth.

There are several **theories** to explain how so many fish species could have become extinct at one time. Some scientists believe the climate became too cold for the fish living in shallow water. Other scientists think the climate became too hot.

The lamprey eel is a jawless fish. The jawless fish have been alive for 500 million years. This type of fish has survived many changes in Earth's climate.

Cod are a popular food source. Due to overfishing, many species of cod are in danger of becoming extinct.

Still other scientists believe the seas "turned over." This means that the cold, low-oxygen water in the deep sea was brought to the surface of the oceans. A new theory suggests that a **meteorite**, much like the meteorite that crashed into Earth at the end of the Cretaceous Period, hit Earth and brought about the extinction of the shallow water fish.

Whatever caused the extinction of fish such as the placoderms, it did not affect the land animals alive at the time. This is a mystery that scientists are still trying to solve.

CHANGING TASTES

The popularity of certain sea animals can change over time. One hundred years ago in North America, lobsters were ground up and put on fields as fertilizer. Now, lobsters are a very expensive luxury food.

Fish in Folklore

The underwater world is mysterious to many people. There are many stories about monsters and mysterious creatures that live underwater. The creatures in many ancient myths have been identified as underwater animals by scientists. Despite such scientific explanations, people still cling to the possibility that monsters and strange creatures live underwater.

Mermaids have been a part of folklore for centuries. There are tales, legends, art, and even movies, such as Disney's *The Little Mermaid*, about mermaids.

Plesiosaurs were marine reptiles, not dinosaurs or fish. They lived during the Mesozoic Era. Plesiosaurs were air-breathing meat-eaters.

The search is still on for Scotland's Loch Ness monster. Scientists have tried for years to find the giant creature that is believed to live in Loch Ness. Using submarines and other equipment, they have learned that Loch Ness is a very deep lake and that it may be linked to the sea. Some people believe that the Loch Ness monster exists and that it is an ancient plesiosaur that hides in deep caves or swims out to the ocean.

IS IT SAFE TO GO INTO THE WATER?

The American movie *Jaws* was about a shark that ate people. This movie made many people fear sharks. However, it is sharks that should fear people. People have killed so many sharks that many shark species are almost extinct.

Digging for Fish

Fossils of fish have been found in almost every country in the world. Every year, new fish fossils are discovered. This map shows some exciting fish and other fossil discoveries.

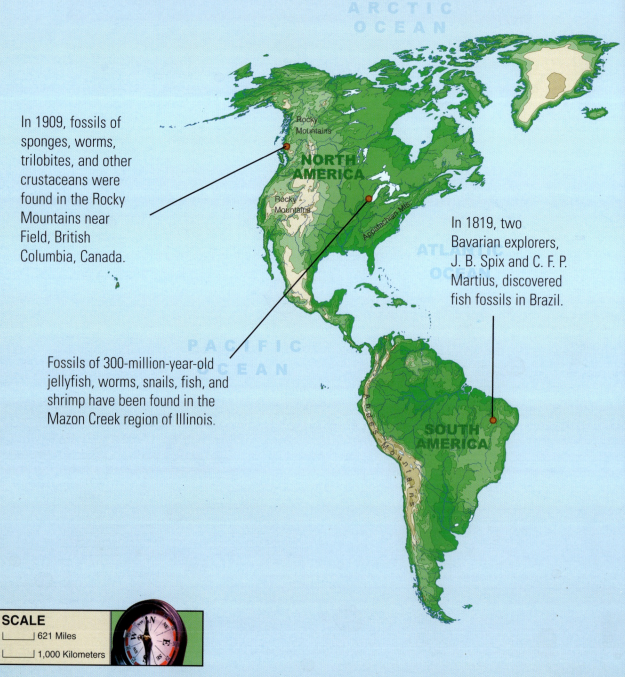

In 1909, fossils of sponges, worms, trilobites, and other crustaceans were found in the Rocky Mountains near Field, British Columbia, Canada.

In 1819, two Bavarian explorers, J. B. Spix and C. F. P. Martius, discovered fish fossils in Brazil.

Fossils of 300-million-year-old jellyfish, worms, snails, fish, and shrimp have been found in the Mazon Creek region of Illinois.

SCALE
621 Miles
1,000 Kilometers

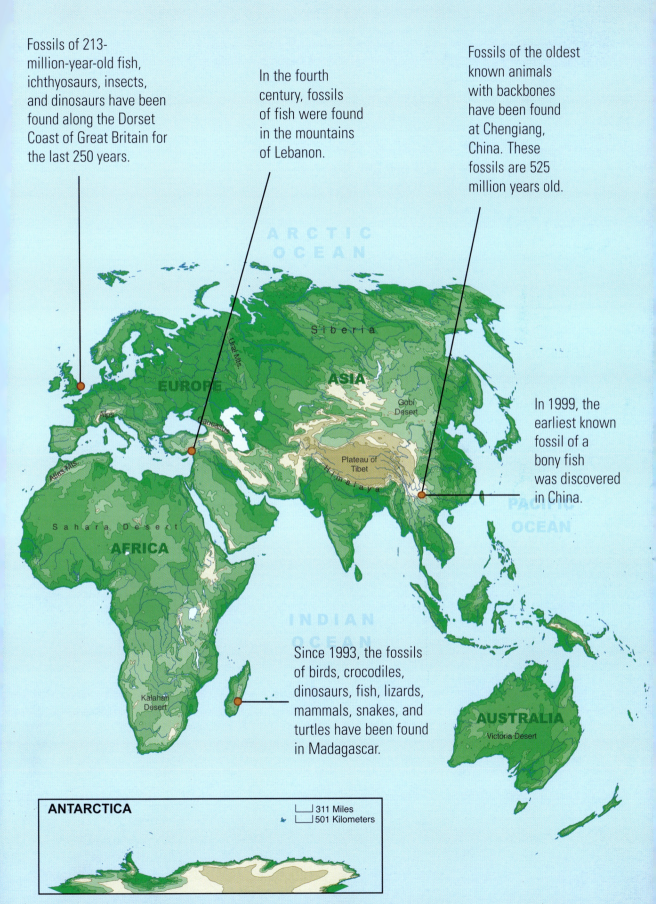

Further Research

WEB SITES

To learn more about prehistoric animals, visit:
http://www.kidsolr.com/science

To learn about paleontology and prehistoric life, visit:
http://www.enchantedlearning.com

To tour a museum that displays interesting prehistoric animals, visit:
http://www.tyrrellmuseum.com/home

BOOKS

Bright, Michael. *Endangered and Extinct: Prehistoric Animals.* Brookfield, CT: Copper Beech Books, 2001.

Cosson, M. J. *Sea Monsters: Myth and Truth.* Logan, IA: Perfection Learning, 2000.

Dipper, Frances. *Extraordinary Fish.* New York: DK Publishers, 2001.

Zimmerman, Howard. *Beyond the Dinosaurs! Sky Dragons, Sea Monsters, Mega-Mammals, and Other Prehistoric Beasts.* New York: Atheneum Books for Young Readers, 2001.

Ancient Activity

Sturgeon

The cod, razorback sucker, and sturgeon are three endangered fish in North America. Research these animals, and present a report to your class. Try to answer the following questions when you write your report:

◆ Which organizations are trying to help the cod, razorback sucker, and sturgeon?

◆ Has the government had an effect on these fish populations?

◆ What human activities have had an effect on these fish?

◆ What is being done to save them?

◆ Do you think people will be able to save the cod, razorback sucker, and sturgeon?

Quiz

♦ ♦ ♦ ♦ ♦ ♦ ♦

Based on what you have read, answer the following questions:

1. Name four theories that explain the extinction of fish at the end of the Devonian Period.
2. When do human beings look like bats?
3. Why did some fish evolve lungs? What did these lungs lead to in later animals?
4. How did the first fish eat?
5. Are young fish born live, or do they hatch from eggs?
6. Name a famous sea monster.
7. Name three ways fish adapted to periods of drought.
8. Are whales and dolphins fish?

1. Earth's climate became too cold. Earth's climate became too hot. The sea "turned over." A meteorite hit Earth.
2. Human beings look like bats and other mammals when they are only a few weeks old in their mother's womb.
3. Fish evolved lungs during dry times. These lungs evolved into swim bladders in later fish and into lungs in amphibians.
4. The first fish filtered food out of the mud on the ocean floor.
5. Most fish hatch from eggs. Only a few species of sharks keep the eggs inside them until the young are ready to be born.
6. The Loch Ness monster
7. Lungs, walking across land to other ponds, burrowing into mud to hibernate until it rains
8. No. Whales and dolphins are mammals.

Glossary

adapted: adjusted to different conditions or environments

amphibians: animals that can live in the water or on land

cartilage: a firm material that is not as rigid as bone

cold-blooded: animals that do not make their own heat

embryo: an unborn animal in the early stages of its development

extinct: no longer alive anywhere on Earth

fertilizes: joining male and female cells so that young begin to develop

fishers: people who catch fish for food or sport

fossils: the rocklike remains of ancient animals and plants

hibernation: being in an inactive state

import: to bring something new into a country

incubated: kept warm

meteorite: a body of rock from outer space that has reached Earth

paleontologists: scientists who study prehistoric life

plankton: very tiny animals and plants that live in water

predators: animals that catch and eat other animals

reptiles: cold-blooded land animals such as lizards

sedimentary rocks: rock that has formed from smaller rocks, and has been compressed over time

species: a group of animals that are similar and can breed together

theories: explanations developed to help explain an opinion or idea

womb: the place inside a mother animal where a young animal lives before it is born

Index

agnathans 7, 14, 15
amphibians 8, 11

bony plates 4, 17

carp 17
cartilage 4, 14, 15, 16, 17
chondrichthians 7, 14, 15
Coelacanth 9, 12, 17
cold-blooded 5

Devonian Period 6, 8
  15, 17, 22
dolphins 5

embryo 13
embryologist 13
era 6, 7
extinction 22, 23

food web 20, 21
fossil 5, 6, 10, 11, 12, 17
  20, 26, 27

gills 5, 13, 15

lamprey eel 22
lobsters 23
Loch Ness monster 25
lungs 5, 8

Megalodon 17

osteichthians 7, 14, 15

Paleozoic Era 6, 7, 8, 16
Pangaea 8
periods 6
placoderms 7, 14
  15, 16, 23
Precambrian Era 6, 19

rays 7, 14, 15
razorback sucker 17, 29
reptiles 6, 8, 25
Rodinia 8

seahorse 19
sharks 4, 5, 7, 11, 14, 15
  17, 18, 20, 25
swim bladder 15

whales 5, 7

Westminster Community Charter School
Library Media Center
24 Westminster Ave.
Buffalo, New York 14215